Contents

About tunnels

It is exciting to speed through a long, dark tunnel in a car or train. But have you ever wondered how this amazing underground passageway was made? Tunnels can go almost anywhere – under roads, railways or bustling city streets, even right through massive mountain ranges and deep under wide rivers!

Structure around a hole

A tunnel is a type of structure. A structure is an object built to resist a push or pull. A tunnel is a structure because it supports the thousands of tonnes of rock, earth or water above it, stopping them falling or flooding into the tunnel. This might seem confusing, because a tunnel is a hole! But it is the roof and sides of the tunnel that make up its structure. They also keep it waterproof.

Building a tunnel is often a difficult job that can take several years. Tunnel diggers and their machinery work in hot and dangerous conditions hundreds or thousands of metres underground. So why do we build tunnels and how are they built?

The Channel Tunnel runs under the sea between England and France. It is the second longest rail tunnel in the world (50.45 km) and took 8 years to build.

Tu S

Chris Oxlade

H www.heinemann.co.uk
Visit our website to find out more information about **Heinemann** Library books.

To order:
☎ Phone 44 (0) 1865 888066
🖹 Send a fax to 44 (0) 1865 314091
💻 Visit the Heinemann Bookshop at www.heinemann.co.uk to browse our catalogue and order online.

First published in Great Britain by Heinemann Library, Halley Court, Jordan Hill, Oxford OX2 8EJ
a division of Reed Educational and Professional Publishing Ltd.
Heinemann is a registered trademark of Reed Educational & Professional Publishing Ltd.

OXFORD MELBOURNE AUCKLAND JOHANNESBURG BLANTYRE
GABORONE IBADAN PORTSMOUTH (NH) USA CHICAGO

Designed by Celia Floyd
Illustrations by Barry Atkinson
Originated by Repro Multi Warna
Printed by Wing King Tong in Hong Kong

ISBN 0 431 10973 7 (hardback)
05 04 03 02 01
10 9 8 7 6 5 4 3 2 1

ISBN 0 431 10980 X (paperback)
05 04 03 02 01
10 9 8 7 6 5 4 3 2 1

British Library Cataloguing in Publication Data

Oxlade, Chris
   Tunnels. – (Building amazing structures)
   1. Tunnels – Design – Juvenile literature
   2. Tunnelling – Juvenile literature
   I. Title
   624.1'93

Acknowledgements

The Publishers would like to thank the following for permission to reproduce photographs:
Ann Ronan Picture Library pp. 7, 26, 29; Associated Press p. 27 (Patrick Gardin); J Allan Cash p. 8; James Davis Travel Photography p. 11; Massachusetts Turnpike Authority, USA p. 23; QA Photos Ltd pp. 4, 12, 14, 16, 18, 19, 20, 25; Robert Harding p. 5; Science Photo Library p. 21; Taylor Woodrow p. 22.

Cover photograph reproduced with permission of QA Photos Ltd.

Every effort has been made to contact copyright holders of any material reproduced in this book. Any omissions will be rectified in subsequent printings if notice is given to the Publisher.

Words appearing in the text in bold, **like this**, are explained in the Glossary.

Why do we build tunnels?

You have probably travelled through many tunnels, on foot, in cars, buses and trains, and perhaps in boats. Transport is one of the main reasons for building tunnels. A tunnel through a hill or mountain creates a short cut. It saves travelling around a hill or climbing over a twisting, snowy mountain pass. A tunnel under a river or **strait** saves time travelling on a ferry. In city centres, tunnels allow trains to move efficiently under the busy streets.

Some tunnels carry water from **reservoirs** to towns and cities. Tunnels called penstocks are also built to carry water from reservoirs to **hydro-electric power** stations. Miners dig tunnels to reach deposits of **minerals** under the ground.

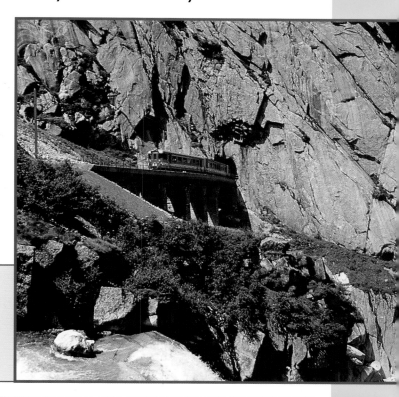

Railway tunnels allow trains to travel at high speed through mountains or beneath roads.

FACTS ✦ It's a tunnel world record!

- Longest tunnel: Delaware Aqueduct, New York State, USA. Water supply tunnel. Completed 1965. Length: 169 km.
- Deepest tunnel: Hitra Tunnel, Norway. Road tunnel. Completed 1994. Depth: 264 m below sea level.
- Biggest tunnel: Yerba Tunnel, San Francisco Bay, USA. Road tunnel. Completed 1936. Dimensions: 24 m wide, 17 m high.

Tunnels in the past

Tens of thousands of years ago many people lived in caves. They probably made their caves larger by chipping away at the rocks, and might have joined caves together with tunnels. The first tunnels we know about were built by ancient civilizations, such as the Egyptians, about 4000 years ago.

Tunnels in ancient times

Ancient people built tunnels for water supply. The tunnels were parts of **aqueducts**, structures that carried water from lakes and rivers to where it was needed for drinking and for **irrigating** crops. The tunnel builders had no machines or explosives. They broke the rock at the **tunnel face** with hammers and chisels. Another method they used was to heat the rock with fire to make it expand and then cool it quickly with water to make it crack.

In ancient times being a tunneller was a very nasty job. It was hot, dusty and extremely dangerous. Most tunnellers were slaves, and hundreds or thousands were killed by rock falls during the building of each tunnel.

FACTS ✦ Amazing ancient tunnels

- The **Babylonians** built a pedestrian tunnel nearly 1 km long under the Euphrates River in modern-day Iraq, in about 2180 BC.
- The Ancient Greeks drove a water-supply tunnel more than 1 km long and 2 m across through limestone on the island of Samos.
- Starting in AD 41, Roman **engineers** built a tunnel 6 km long to drain a lake. The job took 30,000 workers 10 years.

The Hoosac Tunnel, Massachusetts, USA (1851–75), was built using explosives and hand tools.

Tunnels for transport

In the 17th century, industry began to grow in Europe and canals became important for moving materials such as coal or timber. Tunnels were needed to take canals through hills. They were difficult to dig, but cheaper than building flights of **locks** to go over the hills. Dozens of canal tunnels were dug in Europe and North America, starting with one on the Canal du Midi in France, completed in 1692.

In the 19th century, more tunnels were needed as new railway networks were built. By this time, high-power explosives and efficient **pneumatic** drills had made tunnelling through rock much quicker than before. Tunnel builders began **blasting** their way through some of the world's great mountain ranges, such as the Alps in Europe and the Rockies in North America. From the 1820s, a new invention, called the **tunnelling shield**, made it possible to dig safely through soft, water-logged ground under rivers. The shield supported the ground, stopping it caving in as the tunnellers dug.

Types of tunnel

Looking from the inside, all tunnels are really long, thin holes under the ground. The name that **engineers** give to a type of tunnel depends on the ground that it goes through and the method used to build it.

Going underground

Bedrock is solid rock which reaches many kilometres into the Earth. In hills and mountains, bedrock often appears at the surface, but in valleys there are normally thick layers of soft sand, mud or clay on top of the bedrock, which tunnel engineers call soft ground. There is always some water in the ground, too. At a certain depth soft ground is completely **waterlogged**. Even solid rock has cracks in it called fissures that water runs through.

Rock tunnels are tunnels built through solid bedrock. These tunnels are normally found in hills and mountains. Soft-ground tunnels are tunnels built through soft, crumbly rocks or soft ground, such as mud or clay. **Subaqueous** tunnels are underwater tunnels built under rivers and **straits**.

This tunnel in Norway protects the railway track and trains from being buried by avalanches.

These are cross-sections of the four main types of tunnel.

rock tunnel   soft-ground tunnel   cut-and-cover tunnel   immersed-tube tunnel

Mechanical moles and explosives

There are four main ways of building a tunnel. In a rock tunnel, rock is removed by **blasting**. In soft rock or soft ground, a tunnel-boring machine called a **mole** cuts the tunnel. A cut-and-cover tunnel is made by digging a trench in the surface and covering it over with a roof. An immersed-tube tunnel is made by laying a tube along a river or sea bed.

Building a tunnel by blasting or with a mole is called driving a tunnel. Work takes place at the tunnel **heading**, where rock or soil (called **spoil**) is removed from the **tunnel face**, and carried backwards out of the tunnel. Supports are built to stop rock or soil from above falling into the freshly dug section of tunnel. A big mole can produce enough spoil to fill a wheelbarrow every two seconds. The Channel Tunnel moles dug out 8 million cubic metres of spoil – enough to fill nearly 100,000 railway wagons!

Shapes and structures

The hole made by a tunnel is called a **bore**. Tunnels made up of just one bore are called single-bore tunnels. Tunnels with two bores are called twin-bore tunnels.

The bigger the bore of a tunnel, the more difficult the tunnel is to build. Ten metres is about the maximum size practical. It is often easier and quicker to build a twin-bore tunnel with small bores than a single-bore tunnel with a large bore. Twin-bore tunnels have passages connecting the two bores, and sometimes a small **service tunnel** lies between them.

connecting tunnel

main bore

walkway

service tunnel

rail track

main bore

The diagram shows a twin-bore tunnel, with two main bores and a service tunnel, or bore, between them.

Special shapes

If you look at the **portal** of a long road or railway tunnel, you normally see a horseshoe shape. Tunnel bores that go deep underground have an arched roof like this because an arch is a very strong shape. It carries the massive weight of the rock and soil above the tunnel down around the sides and into the ground below.

This road tunnel in Switzerland shows the typical strong, arched shape of a tunnel bore.

Supports for safety

Rock and soil can fall from the roof and walls of an unsupported tunnel, which is dangerous for the tunnellers and delays tunnelling. If the ground is soft, it can slump down, causing **subsidence** at ground level, which can damage the foundations of any buildings above the tunnel. So the tunnel roof and walls normally need to be supported with a tunnel **lining**. The lining holds any loose rock or soil in place, stops the ground above the tunnel from sagging, and stops water from leaking into the tunnel from the ground.

TRY THIS

Tunnel shapes

Cut two pieces of card, each 10 cm x 10 cm. Fold one into a square-shaped tube and curl the other into a circular tube. Lay the tubes in the bottom of an old tray or shoe box. Carefully cover the centre of the tubes with sand or soil. Which tube keeps its shape best, and so would be best for a tunnel?

11

Tunnel materials

A tunnel will only be strong and watertight if **engineers** choose the correct materials. The most important for building modern tunnels are concrete and steel. These are two truly amazing materials.

Uncrushable concrete

Concrete is the most widely used construction material. The ingredients of concrete are **cement**, water and aggregate, which is made up of sand and gravel. When the ingredients are first mixed, the concrete is runny. The cement and water react together and then harden to make a solid which holds the aggregate together. Normal concrete takes several hours to harden and about a month to reach its maximum strength.

Concrete is a good construction material because it is quite cheap and immensely strong. In fact, a mug-sized piece of concrete could support a 30-tonne truck. It can easily be shaped by pouring it into moulds before it sets.

Shotcrete is special concrete that can be sprayed onto tunnel walls, where it sticks and sets.

Tunnelling machinery is lifted by a crane so it can be lowered down a huge **shaft** to the tunnel **heading**.

Super-strong steel

Steel is an **alloy** made mostly of iron. Steel is used to make tunnel **linings** and temporary supports for tunnel walls and roofs. Steel must be protected from water to stop it from **rusting**. This is done by applying a waterproof layer of plastic or by **galvanizing** the steel.

Concrete is only strong when you try to squash it. If stretched, it cracks quite easily. Steel is immensely strong when it is stretched. For example, a steel cable as thick as your finger could support a 30-tonne truck. So where part of a structure made from concrete will be stretched, steel is added. This new material, made up of concrete and steel bars, is called reinforced concrete.

Double-quick setting

In the future, concrete for tunnel linings may be built with a completely new type of concrete, made with **resins** or **polymers** instead of cement. The new concrete would be more expensive, but it would set within a few minutes, allowing tunnellers to dig more quickly.

concrete slab

steel reinforcement

This simple reinforced concrete slab might be used in the roof of a cut-and-cover tunnel.

Designing a tunnel

An organization decides that it needs to build a tunnel. For example, a railway company wants to construct a tunnel to reduce journey times for its trains. But before the actual construction of the tunnel begins, much time will be spent on planning and designing it, with many experts brought in to help at every stage of the project. The first decision to make is how many **bores** the new tunnel needs, and how big the bores should be.

This diagram clearly shows how the Channel Tunnel links England and France.

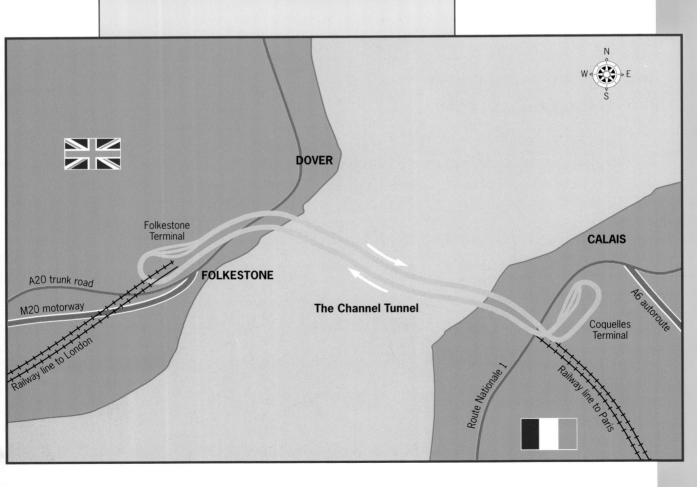

DOVER

CALAIS

Folkestone Terminal

FOLKESTONE

A20 trunk road

M20 motorway

The Channel Tunnel

Coquelles Terminal

A6 autoroute

Railway line to London

Route Nationale 1

Railway line to Paris

Which way?

The easier it is to build a new tunnel, the cheaper it will be. This means avoiding rocks and soil that will be difficult and costly to tunnel through. So a **geological survey** of the ground on the planned route is carried out by a specialist **engineer**. The route of a tunnel must also avoid the foundations of buildings and other underground services, such as sewers and gas mains.

During this geological **investigation**, **boreholes** are dug and samples of the rocks and soils are tested to see how strong they are. The amount of water in the ground is also measured. The route of the tunnel might be changed if weak rock or lots of water are found.

After the investigation the details of the tunnel are worked out and drawings are made. The designer gives the tunnel builder all the information needed to build the tunnel, such as the tunnel's route, its size, and the materials to use.

New uses for tunnels

Transport tunnels create a clear path for vehicles and trains, and help to reduce environmental problems, such as noise and exhaust fumes. In the future, as tunnelling techniques improve, new roads and railways might run through rock tunnels deep underground. Cities could be linked by high-speed underground transit systems, with vehicles travelling at more than 500 km per hour.

Site preparation

Building a long road or railway tunnel is an enormous construction project that can take several years. Normally one **engineering** company, called the main contractor, organizes the whole construction job. There are also dozens of smaller companies called sub-contractors, who do special jobs such as **blasting**, **surveying**, or supplying concrete. Before construction of the tunnel itself can start, the construction site must be made ready.

Digging from both ends

Tunnels are normally dug from both ends at once. Where possible, **shafts** are dug down from the surface so that **spoil** can be removed up through them instead of back along the tunnel itself.

Digging sometimes starts from the middle of the tunnel, too. Machinery and materials are lowered down a huge shaft from the surface. At the French end of the Channel Tunnel, a shaft 55 m across and 75 m deep was dug.

Sections of tunnel **lining** are lowered into the Channel Tunnel for transport by train to the tunnel heading.

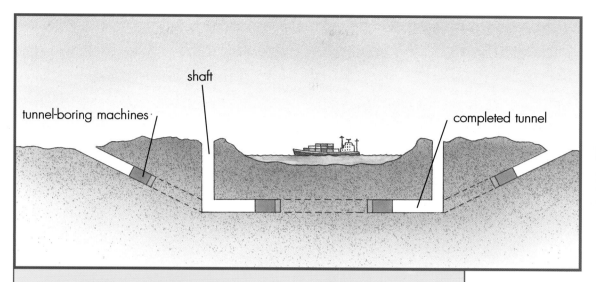

This shows how four tunnel-boring machines can be used to dig an underwater tunnel.

Fighting floods

Water is a big problem for tunnel builders. It can flow in unexpectedly as a tunnel is dug, carrying sand or mud with it. In some tunnels there have been inflows of more than 250,000 litres – enough to fill five bath tubs every second. This is dangerous for workers, and sometimes buries machinery and stops the tunnelling. Engineers often drill **boreholes** from the surface along the line of the tunnel to lower the **water table**. They can also pump **grout** into the ground, which sets, filling gaps in the rock or soil that water could flow through.

FACTS ✚ Under pressure

One way of stopping water from flowing in is to pressurize the tunnel. An airtight seal is placed behind the tunnel **heading** and air is pumped into the heading. The increased **air pressure** tries to push water back into the rocks.

Boring in soft ground

In soft rocks, a tunnel-boring machine or **mole** bores through the rock. The **tunnel face**, roof and sides must be supported to stop them collapsing as digging progresses. So as the mole moves forwards, cutting at the tunnel face, a tunnel **lining** is added behind it. The tunnellers must always be prepared for the unexpected, such as ground containing water, or a layer of hard rock.

Mega moles

A mole is shaped like a cylinder. The cylinder has the same diameter as the tunnel **bore** it digs. At the front is a rotating circular cutting head, with hard metal teeth that scrape away the rock. The cutting head is pushed forwards by **hydraulic rams**. Behind the cutting head the cylinder supports the tunnel roof and sides. Machinery just behind

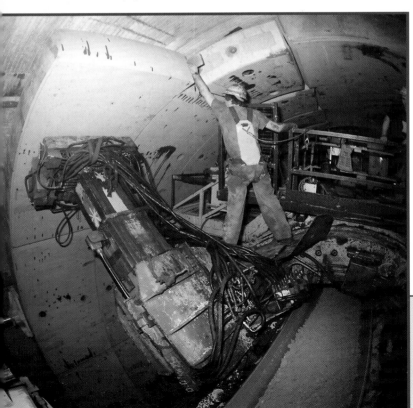

the cylinder lifts sections of lining into place. Moles for major transport tunnels are gigantic machines. The largest Channel Tunnel machine weighed 1575 tonnes, was 8.75 m across and twice the length of a soccer pitch!

Here, a section of tunnel lining is being placed. Spoil is being removed by the **conveyor**.

This is one of the massive Channel Tunnel tunnel-boring machines. The cutting head is on the left.

Moles on the move

As a mole cuts through the ground, **spoil** falls through holes in the cutting head. It is carried on a conveyor belt to trucks or railway wagons which carry it out of the tunnel. Modern moles can dig through rock such as chalk at up to 200 m a day. That doesn't sound much, but it would take a person about two months to do the same amount of digging.

The mole is steered to make the tunnel turn left or right and to move towards the surface or deeper underground. Some moles are steered automatically by a laser beam fired along the tunnel, which gives the mole a perfectly straight line to follow.

TRY THIS

Catastrophic collapses

Make a pile of sand (or soil) at least 10 cm high outdoors on a flat surface. Try digging a circular tunnel a few centimetres wide through the sand. Use a small stick to dig away the sand. Can you see how the roof and walls collapse? The wider you try to make the tunnel, the worse the collapses become. The cylinder of a tunnelling mole stops this happening.

Digging into rock

Tunnels through hard rock are driven by **blasting** away the rock at the **heading** with explosives. Because the rock is solid, the roof and walls of the new tunnel support themselves. But the blasting often weakens the rock around the tunnel, so tunnel **lining** is normally added for strength and to stop loose pieces of rock falling into the tunnel.

Explosives are placed in drilled holes before being detonated by electricity – at a safe distance.

Blasting and mucking

Tunnel builders carry out the blasting process in a cycle which is repeated again and again. The first stage is to drill several deep holes into the **tunnel face** using **pneumatic** drills. The drills are mounted on a vehicle called a jumbo. When the holes are deep enough, the jumbo is moved back down the tunnel and explosive charges are put in the holes. The workers move a safe distance away and the charges are detonated with electric **fuses**.

A **ventilation** system pumps dust and fumes created by the explosions out of the tunnel. A mechanical loader picks up the rubble and puts it on to a conveyor belt, which carries it to waiting trucks or railway wagons. Removing the rubble is called mucking. The jumbo is moved back into place and the cycle starts again. In hard rock, the tunnel can progress at about 20 m a day.

Drilling and blasting are also used to create vast underground chambers. This cathedral-sized turbine hall of a **hydro-electric power** station is 150 m underground.

A smooth finish

Blasting leaves a jagged tunnel, often with loose pieces of rock. So as the heading moves forward, the tunnel roof and walls are supported with steel arches or **shotcrete**. Later a concrete lining is added. Steel or wooden moulds called formwork are placed around the roof and walls and concrete is pumped behind them. When the concrete is set, the formwork is removed, leaving a smooth lining. Steel roof supports are also used in mining tunnels, which may be dug by blasting or by hand-held drilling machines.

In hot water

Tunnels through mountains often go through **bedrock** thousands of metres below the mountain tops. In these deep tunnels, the rocks and any water in them can be hot, creating extra problems for tunnellers. For example, during the building of the Simplon railway tunnel, which travels more than 2000 m under the Alps between Italy and Switzerland, tunnellers had to cope with scalding hot water at 54°C flowing into the workings.

Ready-made tunnels

Tunnel builders think of driving tunnels underground with **moles** or explosives as true tunnelling, because the rock and soil above the tunnel stay in place. Two other types of tunnels, cut-and-cover tunnels and immersed-tube tunnels, are constructed from above ground instead.

Cutting and covering

The cut-and-cover tunnelling method is used to build tunnels near the surface, such as **pedestrian** subways. There are three stages in building a cut-and-cover tunnel. A trench is dug along the line of the tunnel, the tunnel **lining** is placed in the trench, and then soil is put back on top.

The tunnel lining normally comes in **precast** sections of reinforced concrete, which are lowered into the trench and joined together. Using precast sections speeds up building, which is important because cut-and-cover tunnels are often built in very busy streets.

A cut-and-cover tunnel under construction. The reinforced concrete roof is complete.

Sinking sections

The immersed tube is the newest tunnelling method. It was first used in 1906 for a railway tunnel under the Detroit River, USA. The tunnel is made up of sections of tube joined together to make a long tube that lies on a river or sea bed. The tube resists the huge pressure of water outside. In a river 50 m deep, the pressure is the same as a huge truck resting on every square metre of the tunnel. Think of that next time you go through a tunnel under a river!

To build an immersed-tube tunnel, first, **prefabricated** sections of tube are placed in a trench in the river bed, joined together and weighted down with tonnes of concrete. Next, the tube is covered over with concrete or gravel to protect it.

A section of twin-bore immersed-tube tunnel is moved into position by tugs.

TRY THIS

Pushing a pipe

Another method of tunnelling through soft ground, which is used for small-bore water tunnels, is called pipe-jacking. In pipe-jacking, the tunnel lining itself does the digging. Try this experiment to see how it works. Make a tube about 10 cm long and 5 cm across from card. Push it slowly into a pile of damp sand. After a few centimetres, pull the sand inside the tube out with a small stick. Now push the tube forward again.

Tunnels in use

After construction work on a tunnel is completed, the tunnel is prepared for use. All the construction machinery, such as the **spoil**-removal trucks and digging **moles**, is removed from the site. Sometimes it is easier to leave moles under the ground instead of taking them apart and removing them, especially if the moles have been custom-built (specially built) and would be no good for building another tunnel.

Adding services

In a transport tunnel, the road surface or railway track is laid through the tunnel. Services, such as lighting, electricity, communications and water, are added along the whole length of the tunnel, as well as traffic control lights or railway signals. Emergency equipment, such as fire alarms and **sprinklers**, is placed at regular intervals along the tunnel. Watertight doors, which seal off sections of a tunnel if water floods in, and fireproof doors, are put in place.

Ventilation is also very important. Engine exhaust fumes have to be removed and fresh air supplied for people to breathe. This is done with electric fans and air ducts.

Fresh air first

The first long road tunnel in the world was the Holland Tunnel under the Hudson River in New York, completed in 1927. Its designer, Clifford Holland, had to solve the problem of exhaust fumes from the cars in the tunnel. He did this by installing fans in the tunnel roof and a duct under the roadway. The fans suck polluted air out of the tunnel, which is replaced by fresh air from the duct.

In an emergency...

The biggest danger in transport tunnels is fire. If fire starts in a vehicle or train, the tunnel becomes blocked. Heat from the fire cannot escape upwards and the temperature gets very high. Smoke and fumes also spread quickly along the tunnel. So it is important for tunnel operators and the emergency services to have emergency procedures to evacuate tunnels safely and quickly. These procedures have to be practised regularly so that everybody in the emergency team knows what to do.

These fire crews are practising what they would do in the event of an emergency.

Tunnels that went wrong

Things can always go wrong as a tunnel is built. The tunnel roof or walls can collapse, water can flood in, or unexpected types of rock may be encountered. Accidents can also happen once a tunnel is completed and in use.

Building problems

- LÖTSCHBERG TUNNEL In 1908, water and gravel poured into a **heading** on the Lötschberg Tunnel under the Swiss Alps. More than 1 km of tunnel was filled with debris and 25 tunnellers were killed. They had thought they were digging into **bedrock**, but they had hit soft ground under a river valley.

- TANNA TUNNEL The Tanna Tunnel, a rock tunnel built in the 1920s in Japan, suffered many problems. One surge of water killed sixteen workers and trapped fifteen others, who were dug out seven days later.

- THAMES TUNNEL Water and sand broke through the **tunnelling shield** of the Thames Tunnel in London five times, once drowning six tunnellers.

Water gushes into the heading of the Thames Tunnel, London, in 1828, killing six tunnellers.

- SEIKAN TUNNEL Builders of the Japanese Seikan Tunnel, the world's longest underwater tunnel (54 km), encountered very difficult rock conditions. The tunnel took twice as long to build and cost ten times as much as was planned. Sixty-six workers were killed in accidents.

Problems in use

- MONT BLANC TUNNEL In March 1999, a truck carrying flour and margarine caught fire in the Mont Blanc Tunnel, between Italy and France. Dozens of vehicles came to a stop in the tunnel. At least 39 people died in the fire and from inhaling smoke and fumes. Because of the intense heat it took two days to put the fire out. It is thought that extra air pumped into the tunnel to help people breathe made the fire burn more fiercely.

Shown here are the remains of a fire truck destroyed in the Mont Blanc Tunnel fire in 1999.

- HOLLAND TUNNEL In 1949, a truck carrying flammable chemicals caught fire and exploded in the Holland Tunnel, New York. About 150 m of the tunnel was damaged, and many vehicles were destroyed. But thanks to the **ventilation** system, nobody was killed.

Tunnel facts

The world's longest road tunnels

Length (km)	Tunnel	Year open	
24.5	Laerdal, Norway	2000	
16.9	St Gotthard, Switzerland	1980	
14.0	Arlberg, Austria	1978	
12.9	Pinglin, Taiwan	2000+	
12.9	Fréjus, France/Italy	1980	
11.6	Mont Blanc, France/Italy	1965	

The Laerdal Tunnel takes fifteen minutes to drive through!

The world's longest rail tunnels

Length (km)	Tunnel	Year open	
53.6	Seikan, Japan	1988	
50.45	Channel Tunnel, UK/France	1994	
22.3	Shimitzu, Japan	1982	
19.8	Simplon I	1915	(Italy/Switzerland)
19.8	Simplon II	1921	(Italy/Switzerland)
19.1	Vereina	1999	(Switzerland)

The Seikan Tunnel is also the world's longest underwater tunnel, although the Channel Tunnel has more of its length actually under water.

This is an 1851 design for a tunnel under the English Channel, designed to be built with iron tubes.

FACTS ✢ Tunnelling firsts

- First canal tunnel and first use of explosives: Canal du Midi Tunnel, France. Completed 1681. Length: 155 m.

- First underwater tunnel and first use of **tunnelling shield**: Thames Tunnel, London, England. Completed 1843. Original length: 366 m. Now part of London Underground system.

- The inventor of the tunnelling shield, the **engineer** Marc Isambard Brunel, got the idea for his machine from watching a tiny **mollusc** called a teredo, or shipworm. Brunel watched it boring through wood in its shell, pushing sawdust out behind it.

- First rail tunnel: Mont Cenis, France/Italy. Completed 1871. Length: 13.7 km.

- First use of high explosives and compressed air drills: Hoosac Tunnel, Massachusetts, USA. Completed 1875. Length: 7.6 km. It was the first to use **ventilation**.

- First road tunnel: Holland Tunnel, New York, USA. Completed 1927. Length: 2.6 km.

- First immersed-tube: Detroit River Railroad Tunnel, Ontario, Canada. Completed 1906.

- First alpine road tunnel: Mont Blanc Tunnel, France/Italy. Completed 1965. Length: 11.6 km.

Glossary

air pressure   the pressure made by the air in the atmosphere. Air pressure goes up when air is squeezed into a smaller space.

alloy   material made of a metal and another metal or another substance. For example, steel is an alloy made of iron with a small amount of the substance carbon.

aqueduct   channel that carries water. The channel may be made of pipes, tunnels and bridges. The word aqueduct is also used for a bridge that carries water.

Babylonia   ancient empire which flourished in the second millennium BC in the area known today as the Middle East

bedrock   hard, solid rock that goes deep into the Earth

blasting   breaking up rock using explosives

bore   single hole through the ground. Some tunnels have just one bore, others have two or even three.

borehole   deep, narrow hole bored down into the ground to find out what earth and rocks lie below. Samples of the earth and rocks are taken out of the hole.

cement   powder that hardens into a rock-like substance after it is mixed with water. Cement is an ingredient of concrete.

conveyor   belt or machine to move things on

engineer   a person who designs or builds structures

fuse   short piece of wire which becomes so hot that it melts when a large electric current flows through it. Fuses are used to make explosives ignite.

galvanize   to cover steel with a coating of zinc. The zinc protects the steel from rusting.

geological   to do with the rocks that make up the Earth

grout   mixture of cement and water. It is used to make earth or loose rock waterproof.

heading   area near the tunnel face where tunnelling work is being carried out

hydraulic ram   machinery that has a piston and a cylinder which is filled with liquid. Pumping more liquid into the cylinder makes the piston move in or out.

hydro-electric power   power, normally in the form of electricity, made by letting water from a reservoir flow through a turbine. A generator attached to the turbine creates electricity.

investigation   collecting information, for example about the rocks under the ground

irrigation   collecting water and making it flow to where it is needed to water growing crops

lining   covering on the inside of a tunnel that supports the ground around the tunnel and stops water flowing into the tunnel

lock   a step on a canal that allows ships to move uphill and downhill

minerals   chemicals that rocks are made of. Minerals are often mined for use in industry.

mole   machine that bores through the ground

mollusc   creatures, such as snails, with soft bodies and hard shells

pedestrian   person walking

pneumatic   powered by air

polymer   chemical with very long molecules. Rubber, silk and plastics are polymers.

portal   entrance to a tunnel

precast   concrete that is set into a shape before it is put in place

prefabricated   made from parts built in a factory

reservoir   artificial lake that forms behind a dam

resin   yellow or brown transparent substance, sometimes very hard and sometimes soft and sticky. Sap from a fir tree is a resin.

rust   brown, flaky substance formed when iron reacts with air and water. Rusting weakens iron and steel.

service tunnel   small tunnel next to a transport tunnel that can be used to reach different parts of the tunnel

shaft   hole (normally a vertical hole) leading from the ground to a tunnel below

shotcrete   thick liquid concrete sprayed onto a tunnel wall, where it hardens

spoil   rock or soil dug from a tunnel face

sprinkler   device that sprays water on to a fire

strait   narrow stretch of sea

subaqueous   underwater

subsidence   when the earth or rock underground collapses slightly, so that the surface sinks downwards

surveying   measuring the precise position of places on the ground in a tunnel, or investigating what sort of rocks are under the ground

tunnel face   area of rock or ground at the very end of a tunnel that is dug away as the tunnel is built

tunnelling shield   shield that stops a soft tunnel face collapsing as it is dug away

water table   the top of the layer of ground which is full of water

waterlogged   saturated with water

ventilation   circulation of fresh air

Index